Newborn skin is deli
the baby's immune sy
Chemicals, fragrances
clothing, detergents, and baby products can cause newborn skin irritation, dryness, chafing, and rashes. However, there's much you can do to protect your baby from these skin problems.

Your baby's skin is more delicate, more fragile and more permeable than an adult's.

This recipes will help to relieve dry, itchy skin and the best ways to keep baby's skin healthy.

In my book I will show you how to make cosmetics for your baby easy and fast. You will be able to learn how to make soaps, shower gels, bath bombs, shampoos and bath bombs, that can bring so many joy to your baby while he is taking bath. It can be not only healthy, but aslo very funny and creative!

Tips

To each your creation, you can add natural colorants. It will help your cosmetics to look more «tasty».

A few ideas for natural colorants:

- Green: french green clay, chlorella powder, spinach juice.
- Yellow: finely ground safflower, turmeric, saffran.
- Orange: annatto seed powder, carrot juice, orange peel juice.
- Pink/Red: rose clay, alkanet root powder, beet root powder.
- Purple: black currant juice.
- Blue: starch.
- Brown: cinnamon, cacao powder, coffee.
- White: powdered milk.

Start with about 1/8 teaspoon per pound of soap base. Make sure to mix your colorants with either a tiny bit of water or oil first or even a small amount of soap (in a separate cup) until they are smooth. That way you don't end up with chunks of unmixed powder in your soap.

*all my recipes are without colorants, but you can add some.

Essential oils can be used to add a lovely scent to your creations. But do not forget to use only safe oils for your baby's skin. Some essential oils can cause allergy (citrus, floral...). In my recipes, I use only safe oils.

Peppermint, Rosemary, Rose, Chamomile, Bergamot, Jasmine, Lemongrass, Lavenda, Peach, Melon, Melisa, Vanilla, Patchouli, Ylang Ylang, Eucalyptus, Tea Tree, Orange essential oils.

Avocado, Olive, Jojoba, Almond, Grape seed oils.

Do not use cosmetics longer then one month. Natural cosmetics has very short shelf life.

BATH BOMBS

1. Place the dry ingredients in a bowl and then mix them all evenly with the whisk.

2. In a separate container, mix the liquid ingredients together. Note that in this step, the essential oils, scents and natural colorants are added.

3. Slowly add the liquid mixture to the dry ingredients, one small spoon at a time. Mix.

4. When well mixed, you simply pack this mixture into a bath bomb mold and pack tightly, then let it dry. Work quickly so as not to let the bath bomb mixture dry out.

Lavenda Bath Bombs

- 1 cup baking soda
- 1 cup lemon acid
- 3 ml lavenda essential oil
- 3 ml melon essential oil
- 1 tsp dry lavenda flowers

Mint Bath Bombs

- 1 cup baking soda
- 1 cup lemon acid
- 3 ml mint essential oil
- 3 ml melisa essential oil
- 1 tsp dry mint leaves

Milky Bombs

- 1 cup baking soda
- 1 cup lemon acid
- 3 ml rose essential oil
- 4 ml vanilla essential oil
- 1 tbsp dry goat milk

Herbal Bombs

- 1 cup baking soda
- 1 cup lemon acid
- 2 ml melisa essential oil
- 2 ml mint essential oil
- 2 ml rosemary essential oil
- 1/2 tsp dry chamomile flowers
- 1/2 tsp dry melisa leaves

Chamomile Bombs

- 1 cup baking soda
- 1 cup lemon acid
- 4 ml chamomile essential oil
- 2 ml lemongrass essential oil
- 2 tsp dry chamomile flowers

Rose Bombs

- 1 cup baking soda
- 1 cup lemon acid
- 4 ml rose essential oil
- 3 ml jasmine essential oil
- 1 tsp dry rose flowers
- 2 tbsp bath salt

«Sweet Dreams» Bombs

- 1 cup baking soda
- 1 cup lemon acid
- 2 ml mint essential oil
- 2 ml lavenda essential oil
- 2 ml melisa essential oil
- 2 ml patchouli essential oil
- 2 tbsp bath salt

«Freshness» Bombs

- 1 cup baking soda
- 1 cup lemon acid
- 4 ml mint essential oil
- 2 ml eucalyptus essential oil

«Sweet» Bombs

- 1 cup baking soda
- 1 cup lemon acid
- 4 ml bergamot essential oil
- 2 ml rose essential oil
- 1 ml chamomile essential oil
- 1 tbsp bath salt

«Flora» Bombs

- 1 cup baking soda
- 1 cup lemon acid
- 2 ml jasmine essential oil
- 2 ml rose essential oil
- 1 ml chamomile essential oil
- 1 ml lavenda essential oil
- 1 tsp dry lavenda flovers
- 1 tsp dry rose flowers

Avocado Bombs

- 1 cup baking soda
- 1 cup lemon acid
- 4 ml avocado oil
- 2 ml olive oil
- 1 tsp bath salt

«Good Night» Bombs

- 1 cup baking soda
- 1 cup lemon acid
- 2 ml lavenda essential oil
- 2 ml ylang ylang essential oil
- 2 ml melisa essential oil

BODY CREAMS & LOTIONS

1. Heat butters and beeswax over low heat until melted. Remove from heat.

2. Add juices, liquid oils, essential oils and natural colorants (optional). Stir to combine well.

3. Store in container of your choice and let your baby enjoy perfect body cream.

Nourishing Body Cream

- 50 g coconut butter
- 25 g shea butter
- 25 g cocoa butter
- 1 tbsp aloe vera juice
- 1 tbsp avocado oil
- 5 drops rose essential oil
- 5 drops chamomile essential oil

Lavenda Body Cream

- 50 g cacao butter
- 40 g shea butter
- 1 tbsp beeswax
- 1 tbsp aloe vera gel
- 5 drops vitamin E oil
- 2 tbsp grape seed oil
- 6 drops lavenda essential oil

Floral Body Cream

- 60 g shea butter
- 30 g coconut butter
- 1 tbsp beeswax
- 1 tbsp avocado oil
- 8 drops vitamin E oil
- 3 drops rose essential oil
- 3 drops jasmine essential oil
- 2 drops tea tree essential oil

«Juicy Fruit» Body Cream

- 50 g shea butter
- 40 g mango butter
- 2 tbsp beeswax
- 1 tbsp jojoba oil
- 5 drops vitamin E oil
- 5 drops peach essential oil
- 5 drops melon essential oil

Herbal Body Cream

- 50 g shea butter
- 30 g cacao butter
- 20 g coconut butter
- 8 drops aloe vera juice
- 5 drops chamomile essential oil
- 5 drops lavenda essential oil
- 5 drops melisa essential oil
- 2 drops mint essential oil

«Bed Time» Body Cream

- 50 g shea butter
- 50 g coconut butter
- 1 tbsp beeswax
- 1 tsp aloe vera gel
- 1 tsp vitamin E oil
- 5 drops lavenda essential oil
- 5 drops bergamot essential oil
- 3 drops mint essential oil

«Fresh skin» Body Cream

- 60 g coconut butter
- 30 g shea butter
- 2 tbsp beeswax
- 2 tsp aloe vera gel
- 1 tsp vitamin E oil
- 5 drops mint essential oil
- 5 drops eucalyptus essential oil

«Little angel» Body Cream

- 50 g shea butter
- 30 g cacao butter
- 20 g coconut butter
- 1 tsp vitamin E oil
- 1 tbsp almond oil
- 8 drops vanilla essential oil
- 5 drops rose essential oil

«Sweet Evening» Body Cream

- 50 g shea butter
- 25 g cacao butter
- 25 g coconut butter
- 1 tsp vitamin E oil
- 1 tbsp olive oil
- 5 drops rosemary essential oil
- 5 drops bergamot essential oil

SHAMPOO

Combine all ingredients in a bottle. Shake well to mix all ingredients. And do not forget to shake each time before use.

Chamomile Shampoo

- 50 ml shampoo base or liquid castille soap
- 50 ml distilled water
- 10 drops chamomile essential oil
- 1 tsp avocado oil

Herbal Shampoo

- 50 ml shampoo base or
  liquid castille soap
- 50 ml distilled water
- 5 drops chamomile essential oil
- 5 drops mint essential oil
- 5 drops lavenda essential oil
- 5 drops melisa essential oil

Lavenda Shampoo

- 50 ml shampoo base or
  liquid castille soap
- 50 ml distilled water
- 10 drops lavenda essential oil
- 5 drops bergamot essential oil
- 1 tsp grape seed oil

Coconut Shampoo

- 50 ml shampoo base or
  liquid castille soap
- 50 ml coconut milk
- 5 drops vanilla essential oil
- 5 drops chamomile essential oil
- 1 tsp almond oil

«Flora» Shampoo

- 50 ml shampoo base or
  liquid castille soap
- 50 ml distilled water
- 5 drops rose essential oil
- 5 drops jasmine essential oil
- 3 drops lavenda essential oil
- 5 drops patchouli essential oil

«Good Night» Shampoo

- 50 ml shampoo base or
  liquid castille soap
- 50 ml distilled water
- 8 drops lavenda essential oil
- 6 drops bergamot essential oil
- 5 drops lemongrass essential oil
- 1/2 tsp olive oil

Rose Shampoo

- 50 ml shampoo base or liquid castille soap
- 50 ml distilled water
- 12 drops rose essential oil
- 5 drops rosemary essential oil
- 5 drops vanilla essential oil
- 1/2 tsp grape seed oil

«Freshness» Shampoo

- 50 ml shampoo base or
  liquid castille soap
- 50 ml distilled water
- 10 drops mint essential oil
- 5 drops tea tree essential oil
- 5 drops eucalyptus essential oil
- 1/2 tsp avocado oil

SHOWER GELS

Simply combine all ingredients and mix slowly, then transfer to a squeeze or pump bottle. Enjoy the beautiful scent together with your baby.

«Soft skin» Shower Gel

- 100 ml shower gel base or liquid castille soap
- 50 ml coconut milk
- 10 drops vanilla essential oil
- 5 drops tea tree essential oil

Chamomile Shower Gel

- 100 ml shower gel base or liquid castille soap
- 1 tsp vegetable glycerin
- 10 drops vitamin E oil
- 10 drops chamomile essential oil

«Summer Morning» Shower Gel

- 100 ml shower gel base or liquid castille soap
- 2 tsp vegetable glycerin
- 1 tsp vitamin E oil
- 1 tsp grape seed oil
- 10 drops rose essential oil
- 5 drops jasmine essential oil
- 5 drops orange essential oil

Herbal Shower Gel

- 100 ml shower gel base or liquid castille soap
- 2 tsp vegetable glycerin
- 1 tsp vitamin E oil
- 1 tsp avocado oil
- 5 drops chamomile essential oil
- 5 drops melisa essential oil
- 5 drops lavenda essential oil

«Fresh Evening» Shower Gel

- 100 ml shower gel base or liquid castille soap
- 1 tsp vegetable glycerin
- 1 tsp vitamin E oil
- 1 tsp grape seed oil
- 10 drops lavenda essential oil
- 5 drops mint essential oil

«Honey Bunny» Shower Gel

- 100 ml shower gel base or liquid castille soap
- 1 tsp vegetable glycerin
- 1 tsp vitamin E oil
- 1 tbsp raw honey
- 8 drops melon essential oil
- 5 drops rose essential oil

Lavenda Shower Gel

- 100 ml shower gel base or
  liquid castille soap
- 2 tsp vegetable glycerin
- 1 tsp vitamin E oil
- 1 tsp olive oil
- 15 drops lavenda essential oil
- 5 drops peach essential oil

«Milky Way» Shower Gel

- 100 ml shower gel base or
  liquid castille soap
- 2 tsp vegetable glycerin
- 1 tsp vitamin E oil
- 1 tbsp powdered goat milk
- 10 drops vanilla essential oil
- 5 drops orange essential oil

Aloe Vera Shower Gel

- 100 ml shower gel base or liquid castille soap
- 1 tsp vegetable glycerin
- 1 tsp vitamin E oil
- 1 tbsp aloe vera gel
- 1 tsp avocado oil
- 8 drops mint essential oil

SOAP

1. Melt The Soap Base

To melt the soap base, cut it into chunks and place in a glass measuring cup. You can either use a double boiler or heat it in your microwave for 30 seconds at a time, until it turns to a smooth liquid.

2. Prepare Your Molds. You can try silicone muffin pans, candy molds, paper cups, frozen juice containers… look around your kitchen and get creative! Lightly spraying your mold with a tiny bit of oil and then wiping it smooth, will help with release. (Though I forget as often as I remember and it still usually works out okay.)

3. Add Colors, Scent, Herbs & Flowers.

Now that you have a liquid base to work with – you can do all sorts of things to it! Add ingredients and mix them with your soap base.

If you'd like to add honey and/or oatmeal, try adding two to three teaspoons per pound of soap base. Make sure your soap has thickened up a bit, before stirring the oatmeal in or it will all settle to the bottom of your mold. Poppy seeds and flecks of vanilla bean can be handled the same way.

If you'd like to add herbs, try rubbing the leaves through a fine mesh sieve first, to break them down into a powder of sorts. (You can also use a small coffee grinder.) This will be easier on your drains than larger pieces. To avoid all of your herbs settling to the bottom of your soap mold, let the soap mixture thicken somewhat before stirring them in.

4. Finishing Up!

Once you've colored and added and layered to your heart's content, then it's time to pour your soap into your selected molds. You might notice a few bubbles across the top. If you spritz them with rubbing alcohol, they'll magically disappear!

Once poured, let your soap sit for an hour or so to harden before trying to unmold. If you find it won't come out easily, you can pop it in the refrigerator for a short while and see if that helps, but do that as a last resort. Refrigerating or freezing will make your soap prone to getting beads of moisture on it.

Chamomile Soap

- 100g clear soap base
- 7 drops camomile essential oil
- 1 tbsp dry chamomile flowers
- 1 tsp honey

Mint Soap

- 100g clear soap base
- 1 tsp shea butter
- 1 tsp dry mint
- 5 drops mint essential oil
- 10 drops avocado oil

«Bed Time» Soap

- 100g clear soap base
- 10 drops lavenda essential oil
- 10 drops rose essential oil
- 5 drops mint essential oil
- 1/2 tsp coconut butter

Relaxing Soap

- 100g white soap base
- 3 drops lavenda essential oil
- 3 drops patchouli essential oil
- 1/2 tsp dry lavenda flowers
- 1/2 tsp cocoa butter

«Soft Touch» Soap

- 100g white soap base
- 30 ml goat milk
- 5 drops grape seed oil
- 3 drops tea tree essential oil
- 1 tsp coconut butter

«Milky Dreams» Soap

- 100g white soap base
- 20 ml goat milk
- 5 drops grape seed oil
- 10 drops lavenda essential oil
- 1 tsp shea butter
- 1/2 tsp dry lavenda flowers

«Sunny Day» Soap

- 100g clear soap base
- 10 drops melisa essential oil
- 1 tsp olive oil
- 1/2 tsp grape seed oil
- 1/2 dry melisa leaves

Peach Soap

- 100g clear soap base
- 1/2 tsp shea butter
- 5 drops avocado oil
- 5 drops olive oil
- 5 drops melisa essential oil
- 1 tsp peach essential oil

«Silky Skin» Soap

- 100g white soap base
- 1 tsp grape seed oil
- 1 tsp shea butter
- 5 drops rosemary essential oil
- 5 drops rose essential oil
- 1 tsp wax (natural)

Floral Soap

- 100g white soap base
- 1 tsp chamomile oil
- 1 tsp cocoa butter
- 5 drops rose essential oil
- 5 drops jasmine essential oil
- 2 drops lavenda essential oil

20382739R00045

Printed in Poland
by Amazon Fulfillment
Poland Sp. z o.o., Wrocław